Facing
Terminal
Illness

Facing Terminal Illness

Herald Press
Scottdale, Pennsylvania
Kitchener, Ontario

FACING TERMINAL ILLNESS
Copyright © 1981 by Herald Press, Scottdale, Pa. 15683
Published simultaneously in Canada by
Herald Press, Kitchener, Ont.   N2G 4M5
Library of Congress Catalog Card Number: 80-84364
International Standard Book Number: 0-8361-1948-7
Printed in the United States of America
Design by David Hiebert

81 82 83 84 85 86 10 9 8 7 6 5 4 3 2

Contents

Foreword

For few people was illness a greater invasion of life than for Mark Peachey.

As a pastor and a mission executive, Mark's work required a busy (sometimes hectic) schedule of travel, meetings, correspondence, and personal interviews. Within months after leaving his post as executive secretary of Rosedale Mennonite Missions, he was replaced by three full-time staff persons.

Yet in the midst of efficient administration, Mark never became impersonal. As a young co-worker, I was impressed again and again with his availability, his initiative in friendship with all kinds of people, and most of all by his prayer and vision.

Prayer and vision. By that I mean his frequent

invitations to me and others to pray with him about administrative decisions, personal relationships, or other matters—combined with his joy in visualizing and implementing God's thoughts for the future. Mark was a practical dreamer.

For such an activist to face the possibility, even probability, of an early death from cancer was a massive challenge. The following pages reflect the struggle toward peace of one man of God. The agony of fear within him competes with the ecstasy of faith, and loses.

The battle of terminal illness when it comes is lonely, but God is there. This was Mark's confession of faith.

Richard Showalter
Mechanicsburg, Ohio

The
Invasion

The Invasion

On September 9, 1977, I went to the doctor for a complete physical examination. I was diagnosed as anemic. On September 11, I was admitted to the Methodist Evangelical Hospital in Louisville, Kentucky, for further testing and observation. I was released from the hospital on September 16, told that I had a rare disease known as myelofibrosis. This is a fibrous growth in the bone marrow which prevents the bone marrow from producing red blood cells. On March 6, 1978, I was again admitted to the same hospital for 10 days of treatment because of a flu-like infection that produced a fever up to 104 degrees.

I have developed a new appreciation for the skills of doctors, nurses, and the services of hospitals and laboratories. I have appreciated the straightforwardness of my doctor. In early October 1977, he said to me, "Now, Mr. Peachey, you understand that your illness is in the area of malignancy." On March 16, just before releasing me from the hospital, my doctor told me further, "Now, Mr. Peachey, you understand that there is no known cure for your illness." Statements like these helped me to understand my own frailty, limitations, and mortality in a way that I had never known before. However, for the first 24 hours after each of these announcements, I experienced a struggle with depression.

This is really a new experience for me. Like most people, I was busy with what I thought was important for me to do in life. But suddenly my life was interrupted by something I hadn't planned or anticipated. It changed my outlook completely—the things that I was doing and what I was concerned about.

I freely admit that the adjustment to this new reality in my life was difficult. I was surprised by my reactions. I am still in a learning process. I really wouldn't give up what the Lord has taught me during this detour in my life; yet neither would I have asked the Lord for this kind of experience. It seems like a paradox.

What follows is an account of my struggle during this invasion, along with some reflections which have come from personal study and searching.

Mark Peachey

1.
Life,
A Trust to
Be
Received

Chapter 1

Life, A Trust to Be Received

Knowing that I am suffering from terminal cancer has impressed me in a new way with the seriousness of life.

I recognize even more than before that life and health are a trust from God—a trust to be received gratefully. I cannot afford to take life for granted. My physical life needs to be nourished and cherished (Ephesians 5:29). The implications of all this can get very practical. I am convinced that it is important for me to eat a good balanced diet, and not become hooked on "junk foods."

I see in sharper focus the wisdom of exercising temperance and moderation in all of life, whether in my working or eating habits. I know that God has given our bodies the capacity for meeting emergencies such as illness in the family, a disaster, storm, or flood.

Yet this capacity for endurance and for meeting emergencies lasts only for a short time. It would be foolish for any of us to assume that we can live with four hours of sleep per night just because we were able to do so through a week of emergencies. We must recognize the needs of the body when it comes to food, rest, diet, and exercise.

Some persons, if given the choice, might say that they wish they had come into the world stillborn. But I thank God that in Jesus Christ I can embrace life regardless of the circumstances. I can say, "Thank you, Jesus, for life and health as a trust from You. I want to be faithful to that trust as long as You can give it to me!"

2.
Illness,
A Time for
Listening

Mark Peachey awaiting the diagnosis of his doctor.

Chapter 2

Illness, A Time for Listening

My first awareness of what I later learned was my terminal illness came to me in September 1977. During the summer I felt a little more than the usual fatigue. I finally went to the doctor on Friday, September 9. After about an hour of examination, he said, "You're anemic. We're going to put you in the hospital to find out why. In fact, I want to admit you this afternoon."

"I can't go into the hospital this afternoon," I objected. "This Sunday night I'm scheduled to be at Williamson, West Virginia. I'm to begin a series of Bible studies for a team of Mennonite Disaster Service people who will be working in disaster recovery work in the hills of eastern Kentucky. I can't go to the hospital today. I have plans for this weekend."

"But Mr. Peachey," he said as he looked right at me, "if you listen to me you're going to the hospital, not to West Virginia. I'll give you a choice—either tonight or Sunday. Get this problem taken care of and then you can go on with your Bible teaching."

"Well, doctor, I'll take Sunday night," I told him. And that was the beginning of what seemed to be an invasion into my life.

In this jolt, in this invasion, I turned to the Bible. I read Job and Psalms twice. I read Daniel, Philippians, Romans 8, and James 5. I read a number of other books. There are good books available, I discovered, to help us work through the meaning of illness. I also found help in the counsel of friends. But in prayer and in crying out to God I found my greatest source of strength.

I've heard it said that illness is God's megaphone.

It's like when a father says to his son, "John, will you mow the lawn?"

John says, "Yeah." But John is busy fixing his bicycle. He likes the bicycle better than the lawn mower.

After a bit the father says, "John."

"Yeah," he responds without looking up. Finally father shouts, "John, did you hear me? It's time to mow the lawn."

I see illness as a time when God raises His voice just a little. That's the way it's been for me. I've heard things from God during this time that

I've never heard before—things I needed to hear.

One thing that has amazed me through this experience is how certain Scriptures come to life and speak to me in my circumstances in a new way. Romans 8 is one example, beginning at verse 18:

> I consider that our present sufferings are not worth comparing with the glory that will be revealed in us. The creation waits in eager expectation for the sons of God to be revealed. For the creation was subjected to frustration, not by its own choice, but by the will of the one who subjected it, in hope that the creation itself will be liberated from its bondage of decay and brought into the glorious freedom of the children of God.
>
> We know that the whole creation has been groaning as in the pains of childbirth right up to the present time. Not only so, but we ourselves, who have the firstfruits of the Spirit, groan inwardly as we wait eagerly for our adoption as sons, the redemption of our bodies. For in this hope we were saved. But hope that is seen is no hope at all. Who hopes for what he already has? But if we hope for what we do not yet have, we wait for it patiently.
>
> In the same way, the Spirit helps us in our weakness. We do not know what we ought to pray, but the Spirit himself intercedes for us with groans that words cannot express. And he who searches our hearts knows the mind of the spirit, because the Spirit intercedes for the saints in accordance with God's will.
>
> And we know that in all things God works for the good of those who love him, who have been

called according to his purpose. For those God foreknew he also predestined to be conformed to the likeness of his Son, that he might be the firstborn among many brothers. And those he predestined, he also called; those he called, he also justified; those he justified, he also glorified.

Shall trouble or hardship, or persecution, or famine, or nakedness, or danger, or sword, my myelofibrosis, or cancer, or hospitalization, or loss of a job—and you can go on and on—shall these things separate us from the love of God?

No, in all these things we are more than conquerors through Him who loved us. For I am convinced that neither death nor life, neither angels nor demons, neither the present nor the future, nor any powers, neither height nor depth, nor anything else in all creation, will be able to separate us from the love of God that is in Christ Jesus our Lord.

To me, this is one of the most powerful and precious Scriptures regarding the Christian's response to illness that I have ever read. It has taken on new meaning for me these past six months.

Now, I do want to comment on verse 28. The King James Version says that "all things work together for good." In later translations (and the Greek supports it), instead of "things" being the subject of that sentence, "God" is the subject. In all things *"God works"* and He works for the good. But "good" must be understood in terms of what God sees to be good. We tend to interpret

24

good in terms which seem good to us—that which is for our pleasure or convenience or comfort, that which we would like to do and be. But it says "for good" from God's point of view.

For those who do what? Those who love him. There's another qualification. How much do I really love God or how much is my affection going out to something else?

Another qualification is, "To those who are called according to His purpose." God has a purpose for me, and He is at work for my good to accomplish that purpose in all circumstances.

We do not need to make God the Author of circumstances in order to feel good about our experiences. Some circumstances come into our lives that are contrary to His purpose, but He is there to work His purpose in us in spite of the circumstances (Philippians 4:11-13).

During serious illness one faces questions such as these: Did I bring this illness upon myself? Is this a chastisement from the Lord as we read in Hebrews 12:1-13? Is this an attack from Satan? Or is it simply an indication of my mortality? Does this mean new directions for what remains of my life and ministry? (See Romans 8:21, Hebrews 9:27, and 1 Corinthians 15:54.)

While it may be well to consider these questions, we must also remember that Paul said in Romans, "How unsearchable his [God's] judgments, and his paths beyond tracing out!" It is important that we learn to be honest with God at times like this.

I used to think that one should not ask the question, "Why?" under such circumstances, but only ask, "What can I learn from this experience?" After reading and rereading Job and Psalms prayerfully, I have changed my mind. To refuse the question "Why?" is to repress one of the basic human emotions. To ask "Why?" out of anger and rebellion, however, is to release one of the most devastating of human emotions (Numbers 14:3).

We cannot avoid asking the question, but we ought not get stuck on it either. One of the doctors in Louisville says that nearly every sick person that comes to his office says, "What did I do that I should have this kind of problem? Why me? Why now?" I don't think we can avoid these "why" questions, but neither should we become preoccupied with them.

Elizabeth Kubler-Ross, in her book *On Death and Dying*, speaks of five stages through which people pass when they face terminal illnesses and possible death. There is the first stage of denial and isolation; the second stage of anger; the third stage of bargaining; the fourth stage of depression; and the fifth stage of acceptance. These reactions may not follow in this exact order for everyone, but I can certainly identify with those feelings in my experience.

Only in time can we look back and understand. But if we are preoccupied in trying to figure out the source of illness, we may not hear the message God has for us as we experience illness.

One painful, but important area to examine is the possibility of a psychomatic or functional illness. Dr. Stanger, president of Asbury Theological Seminary has pointed out that in 1951 approximately 50 percent of the illnesses coming to a doctor's attention were of psychosomatic origin. Today this figure is closer to 80 percent. The pressures of our highly competitive and technological age are taking their toll.

Psychosomatic illness is simply the response of organs within the body to prolonged tensions such as worry, loneliness, fear, despair, anger, conflict, resentment, bitterness, or our inability to cope with whatever pressures life may bring to us. These tensions can produce muscle spasms, colitis, asthma, headaches, ulcers, nausea, and heart pains.

As humans, our capacity for coping with pressure and tension is limited. We may get caught in this type of illness unawares. If we do, it is important to be honest with ourselves, come to the Lord for healing of our spirits and emotions, and seek to deal with our problem. Making ourselves feel guilty for having the problem is not helpful.

Dealing honestly with our problem may require some adjustment in our schedule or work load. It may simply mean coming to the Lord and casting our cares upon Him anew. It may mean confessing our anxieties as sin and finding forgiveness. It may mean renewing our prayer life. We may need to gather a few friends around us (far enough removed from us to be objective, close enough to know our situation) and have them pray for us and give us counsel for further actions.

It is normal to face such a situation in fear, but as Christians we have the resources for courage and hope. There is a way out. When the cause of such an illness is removed, in time the illness leaves also.

Along with asking "Why?" in humble faith and trust in God, we also need to ask, "What can my fellow Christians learn through this experience?"

We have a model in Galatians 4:13 and 14 (NIV) regarding attitudes that should be expressed within the Christian brotherhood during times of illness. Paul writes,

> As you know, it was because of an illness that I first preached the gospel to you. Even though my illness was a trial to you, you did not treat me with contempt or scorn. Instead, you welcomed me as if I were an angel of God, as if I were Christ Jesus himself.

I don't think that God's message through illness is limited only to the person who is sick. I think that God has a message for everyone in the family, in the circle of friends, and in the congregation when illness strikes.

What would you do if someone from your immediate family was diagnosed as having a terminal illness? How would you respond to this?

Could you talk and pray together about it? Could you ask "Why?" in a spirit of love and trust? Could you ask, "What can we all learn from this?" Could you be supportive and pray together for the person who is ill?

We know that no one likes to suffer. I've lived 62 years now, and what little suffering I've had has been a very short part of my life so far. But even if I had been suffering for 62 years, compared to eternity (my whole existence) it would be just a short time. We shouldn't feel too badly if we have to suffer a little in this life, whether it's from persecution or from illness, because in eternity there will be no pain nor sickness.

3.
Healing, A Privilege to Be Sought

Mark Peachey leading a worship service at the
Louisville, Kentucky, Mennonite Fellowship.

Chapter 3

Healing, A Privilege to Be Sought

God can and does heal. He heals through natural processes. When you break a bone, the doctor doesn't heal the bone. He simply sets it and there is in the body a built-in process which does the healing. There is medicine and there is miracle. All healing ultimately comes from God. God is just as great in the natural order as He is in the supernatural order.

While in the hospital, I met a pastor several doors down the hall who had to come to the hospital for surgery because of a hernia. On his church building he had a sign which read, "Jesus Saves and Jesus Heals."

His hernia came from lifting a heavy object onto a small truck. He prayed for his hernia to be healed. He refused to go to a doctor. He prayed and prayed but the pain became more intense. In desperation he said, "If God doesn't heal me, I'm going to tear that sign down from my church. I'm not going to preach one thing and live something else."

Finally, he had a vision which told him that a hernia is like a broken bone. Believing that there was nothing wrong about going to a doctor for a broken bone, he went to a doctor who put him in the hospital for surgery. The doctor said it would have been too late if he had waited much longer.

I had a roommate in the hospital who expressed no regard for God. He had ulcers. For four years he said he could only drink 7-Up or ginger ale at beer parties with his friends. His doctor came across a drug that neutralized the acid which caused the ulcer in his stomach. This semi-retired businessman left the hospital, rejoicing that now he could enjoy his beers and highballs with his buddies as before. His faith was in a miracle drug. His fulfillment was in self-indulgence.

There are many patients whose confidence or "faith" rests only in the tangible—the medicine, surgery, or whatever treatment doctors and hospitals may have to offer. God is not in their thoughts. They have a secular approach to life.

Some Christians feel that using medical services of doctors and hospitals is a denial of their faith, and so they spend a lot of time and energy going to "faith healers" for help.

Out of my experience, study of the Scriptures,

prayer, and reading of various writers, I see no incongruity between faith, trust in God, and fervent prayer on the one hand and the reasonable use of medical services on the other. God is the Author of nature as well as of miracles and uses each according to His purpose. My faith is not in the natural healing processes, not in medicine, not in miracles as such. *My faith is in God, my heavenly Father,* who works through natural processes, who works through medicine, and who works miracles.

It seems since September 1977, when I was anointed and went to the hospital, that the process of further deterioration has stopped. My condition is now described as stable. I'm not sure that I can explain what medicine is doing or whether God is performing a miracle. I just know that God is above nature, medicine, and miracle. I don't care whether He chooses to work through one or all of these processes. I know that all healing and blessing comes from Him. It looks like God is doing some healing in my body. The doctors did say I must be getting help from above.

My faith in God delivers me from the burden of trying to make the distinction between supernatural and natural healing processes, when in my finiteness I can hardly determine which is which. I seem to be living on a thin margin between life and death. Apart from miracle, my days are numbered. I am aware of the subtle temptation to focus my attention on miracle or medicine, rather than resting my faith in God. My faith transcends both medicine and miracle.

Besides physical healing, there is the need for spiritual and emotional healing. My first response to my sudden illness and limitation was much like that of a wild bird trapped in a living room, trying to get out by flying against the glass of the picture window. Again and again the bird bruises its head and wings against the window, as it tries to escape. My wings were bruised, my head was sore.

I struggled with what seemed like two contradictory signals at once. The call to serve at Louisville seemed so clear from God through the church. And now, after 2½ years, when it seemed we had scarcely begun, here was a message from my doctor and evidence in my body that physically something had gone wrong. Why should I be put into a box like this? Where was my heavenly Father in all of this? What did this mean?

A few months before my illness, I had memorized Philippians 1:20 (KJV) and accepted it as a life motto, "According to my earnest expectation and my hope, that in nothing I shall be ashamed, but that with all boldness, as always, so now also Christ shall be magnified in my body, whether it be by life, or by death."

But in my early struggle with my illness, I was unable to say that verse and really mean it when I thought that death might be about as close to me as life. Furthermore, if I would live, I might have the kind of limitations I never experienced before. But as I prayed and sought the Lord, He gave me *spiritual* and *emotional* healing. By His grace I could say, "Yes, Lord, by life or by death." Physical healing seemed much less important! It was tremendous! Psalm 63:3, "Your love is better than life," became very precious to me.

I also see spiritual and emotional healing as the prelude, as the door to prepare me for whatever physical healing God wants to give me. It is more important than physical healing. It places me in a position so that God can give me whatever level of physical restoration He wants to.

For a long time I pondered the question, "Does this illness mean that I am at the end of my earthly pilgrimage, or does it mean that my pilgrimage will need to take on some new dimensions and directions?" It seems that I either wanted to go and be with the Lord or be entirely well so I could do what I wanted to do. Presently, I can keep functioning within limitations by receiving blood transfusions every four to six weeks.

In addition to many who were praying for us, my wife and I sensed a need for a small group to join us in prayer and counsel. We called on friends whom we felt were close enough to know our situation, and yet far enough removed from us to be objective. We were concerned that they would not be praying only on the basis of sentiment, but rather on the basis of trying to understand what God really is saying to us.

Questions such as these were before us:

1. How sick can a pastor be without losing his credibility as a pastor?

2. Can he minister healing to members of the congregation if he himself is ill?

3. Does this whole experience mean early retirement?

4. Should we continue our ministry in Louisville and drop out-of-state administrative responsibilities?

The Lord provided four couples to engage in special prayer for us for about two months. We asked them for counsel to help us understand God's purpose for our lives in this situation, to help us set our priorities, and to pray that God would make me adequate for whatever He had yet for me to do.

As the group was praying and searching, so were we. When we met with the group to receive their counsel, it was exciting to hear that their counsel was in harmony with the thoughts which had developed in our minds as well. The counsel from the prayer group, plus that of several individuals, was confirmed by the fellowship in Louisville. We took this as the Lord's way of helping us to a new sense of direction.

For the present, this meant continuing my ministry in Louisville, dropping other administrative work that has potential for stress and requires traveling, and developing more of a contemplative and reflective lifestyle. We were encouraged to provide more time for writing, counseling, and developing the gifts of younger people in the various ministries of the church.

We are deeply grateful for this new direction and are committed to make the adjustments necessary as God grants strength and opportunity. I believe that God will make me adequate for the work He yet has for me to do and for the person He wants me to become. I find it helpful to think in terms of *reshaping* my life and ministry according to God's purpose, rather than to think about the limitations my illness places upon me. Praise the Lord!

Even in the normal aging process, all of us need to take inventory of our energies and deal with the new expectations our business or church may place upon us. If we can *reshape* our responsibilities periodically, life will hold some exciting adventures which we will surely miss if we remain on the old treadmill.

4.
Death,
A Release
to Be
Accepted

Mark Peachey conversing with his son, Titus
(center), and his son-in-law, Freeman Miller (right).

Chapter 4

Death, A Release to Be Accepted

There are many views these days regarding death. Many persons just ignore it. Others flirt with it. Some say fatalistically, "Whenever my number is called, then I'll go." Still others see death as an escape from the pressures and responsibilities of this life. Some see death as a tragic waste if it occurs before one is 70 or 80 years of age; others are "scared to death" of death. Still others see death as the "healing of eternity."

What does the Lord have to say about death? Hebrews 9:27 states that "man is destined to die once, and after that to face judgment." Hebrews 4 speaks of death as *rest* for the people of God, and calls us to *labor to enter into that rest.* Revelation 14:13 states, " 'Blessed are the dead who die in the Lord from now on.' 'Yes,' says the Spirit, 'they will rest from their labor, for their deeds will follow them.' "

The defeat and sting of death is taken out of death by the resurrected Christ (1 Corinthians 15:54-58). Paul speaks of having the sentence of death within ourselves, "that we might not rely on ourselves but on God, who raises the dead. He has delivered us from such a deadly peril, and he will deliver us. On him we have set our hope that he will continue to deliver us" (2 Corinthians 1:9-10).

Since life is really a trust from God, we trust the Giver of life to take that life unto Himself according to His own wisdom and time. It seems that God chooses to underscore some lives by not removing a handicap, and to place an exclamation point at the end of life for some of His saints by calling them to their eternal rest before their "time is up" according to human reasoning.

One thing we tend to overlook is that when God created this world He didn't make it in a mess. The mess that we are in we have brought upon ourselves. I think it is important that instead of blaming God for illness and pain, we remember we are living in a fallen world. We are here in this bondage of decay. But in Christ there is redemption, not only for the spirit and the soul, but also for the body. When He comes again these bodies will be redeemed. "Who shall change our vile bodies." We will be fashioned according to His glorious body.

Humanly speaking, we would like to have right now all that God has promised in the final redemption. We know our bodies are going to be redeemed and there will be no pain, no sickness, no sorrow in heaven. We cannot support from the Scriptures that we should receive preferential treatment in this life as though we can expect to escape all these sicknesses which we as humans have brought upon ourselves. God said to Adam and Eve, "When you eat of it you will surely die."

We are mortal beings. I am mortal, and I am not sure when in God's plan He is going to say it is time for that mortality to complete its work as far as my life is concerned, and time for me to enter into my rest. The giving and taking of life is in His hand. Praise the Lord!

It is possible for people to shorten their days on earth by violating the laws of good health or by violent measures such as suicide. I find no evidence in Scripture indicating that Satan can take the life of God's saints except as he works through the stupidity and anger of wicked persons. (Note the stoning of Stephen in Acts 7.)

We need to remember that *helplessness does not mean worthlessness* on God's scale of values. God's love is not measured to us according to the volume of our productivity. We are more than a glorified assembly line. We are His children. He loves us because we *are* His children, and He desires our fellowship. It follows then that *being* is more important than *doing*.

Many people who have 20-20 vision and good ears are blind to God's purpose and to the needs of others. They are deaf to the cry of help from their brothers and sisters. Of all handicaps, this kind of blindness and deafness is most pathetic.

Looking to God in the midst of limitations, disappointment, and suffering is an expression of a vibrant faith that survives and thrives under difficult circumstances, *"whether by life or by death."*

I found, as time went on, that I needed to have my mind *delivered* from a morbid subconscious dwelling on my illness. Instead I needed the sanctified imagination to envision God's healing processes at work in me. This took self-discipline on my part, for at the same time there were constant reminders of the illness in my body.

Here is where we need each other, both in the family and the local fellowship. The New Testament places the responsibility for healing ministries within the fellowship and loving relationships of the body of Christ, specifically the local congregation. I am a Christian pastor and pastors are ministers of life. God is calling us to a new *quality* of relationships. Pastors have a tremendous responsibility in sharing, prayer, and counsel to help lead the way. Without that relationship, genuine healing is impossible and illness can be a devastating and isolating experience.

Freedom to talk openly *within the family circle* regarding the nature and effect of serious or terminal illness is also important. Funeral and burial arrangements need to be discussed. This becomes a tremendous therapy for spiritual and emotional healing. Even though it may be painful, even though it may be burdensome at times, we must rise above our fears and pain and be open to talk and pray together. "God did not give us a spirit of timidity, but a spirit of power, of love and of self-discipline." Praise the Lord! This is one way to bear one another's burdens and so fulfill the law of Christ, because "whether we live or die, we belong to the Lord." There is great comfort in this great truth. Thank you, Lord Jesus.

5.
Reflections

Mark Peachey in his study at Louisville, Kentucky.

Chapter 5

Reflections

I wrote the following reflections during my hospitalization, December 26, 1978, to January 11, 1979, and refined them during my later confinement at home. (*Editor's Note:* The last paragraph was written on the day Mark died.)

1. One readily observes that pleasure and pain, joys and sorrows, satisfactions and suffering, fulfillment and disappointment, youth and aging, health and sickness, birth and dying, labor and rest, all seem to be a part of the creation order since the Fall. We read of no unpleasant nor painful experience before the Fall. But God has given us so many pleasant things in life to enjoy even in spite of the Fall.

2. Nevertheless, I am a mortal being. "When you eat of it you will surely die," "cursed is the ground because of you," "man is destined to die once, and after that to face the judgment," and "all have sinned and fall short of the glory of God." "All men are like grass ... the grass withers and the flowers fall." These are but a few of many Scriptures describing the temporary nature of the creation order since the Fall. I guess I am just learning how "grassy" I am. Even though I know that, I do not like when pain, suffering, and disappointments come *my* way.

3. It was into this kind of a fallen and broken world that Jesus came. Isaiah sees Him as the shepherd that "gathers the lambs in his arms." Jesus said "I have come that they may have life, and have it to the full." But this cost Jesus suffering, immense physical and psychological pain—to be rejected of men, to wrestle alone in the garden, and finally to suffer and die on the cross—to accomplish our redemption. Even though He came to earth to "do your will, O God" (Psalms and Hebrews), yet when He came to the specific situation in Gethsemane, He needed again to deal with His desires to find another way. "My Father, if it is possible, may this cup be taken from me. Yet not as I will, but as you will." "Although he was a son, he learned obedience from what he suffered" (Hebrews 5:8).

4. Now I have life in Him. Spiritually and emotionally I am healed and complete in Him. "Though outwardly we are wasting away, yet inwardly we are being renewed day by day." I rejoice in the good health I have had for years. I want to use whatever energies He yet gives me for God's glory. Fellowship and acceptance with God does not rise and fall with my hospitalization or ability to perform my work. This is precious to know. However, each time a new hospitalization or painful situation comes my way, I need to lay fresh hold on God's resources for that experience. "And we know that in all things God works for the good of those who love him" (Romans 8:28).

5. I have a disease in my bone marrow for which there is no known cure. In layman's language, it is cancer of the bone marrow. I am anemic. This makes me vulnerable to various infections and very weak in combating them. I do not understand why I should need to bear these infirmities and limitations. The doctors so far cannot tell me the cause of my cancer. Neither can I. But my life is being refined. I see possibilities of a new kind of ministry for me.

Is God perhaps seeking to teach us all something about the meaning of suffering in an age when we have pretty well learned how to avoid it, both physically and spiritually? We *rejoice* in our redemption in Christ, but *shrink* from the suffering and crossbearing (physically and emotionally) that He endured to procure our redemption. "For it has been granted to you on behalf of Christ not only to believe on him, but also to suffer for him" (Philippians 1:29).

Even though my suffering grows out of an illness instead of from being abused for my faith, my reaction to these interruptions, disappointments, and pain does say something about my faith and does something to my faith in God.

6. All healing comes from God. *All* healing comes from God! God works through natural processes, medicine, and miracle. I continue to pray for healing, both for specific problems such as this phlebitis in my leg and for my cancer. I trust God to hear my prayers. I'm convinced that He does. But I also recognize my mortality and the "grassiness" in my flesh. I know that in Jesus we have a High Priest who is touched with the feelings of our infirmities. God loves and cares. He takes no pleasure in seeing His people suffer. However, as Paul says in Romans 11:33-36:

> Oh, the depth of the riches of the wisdom and knowledge of God! How unsearchable his judgments, and his paths beyond tracing out!
>
> "Who has known the mind of the Lord? Or who has been his counselor?"
>
> "Who has ever given to God, that God should repay him?"
>
> For from him and through him and to him are all things. To Him be the glory forever! Amen.

Jesus prayed in Gethsemane for another way, but He died on the cross the next day. His prayer was heard according to God's purpose for Him. So I trust God to grant me life and health according to *His ways and purpose for me.* He can let nature take its course in my illness. He can intervene in my behalf. He already has. I pray and trust that He may continue to do so. But either way, His grace is sufficient to sustain me and give meaning to it all, provided my faith and trust in him does not falter.

7. I thank and praise God for the privilege of being part of a brotherhood that cares and prays and shares the burden. That is so precious.

Over the past several months, again and again I've anticipated health and freedom from the confines of a hospital bed. Instead I have met the disappointment of a weakened body and uncertainty about my physical capabilities. This cycle of anticipation and disappointment is a difficult one. It is a normal part of many areas of life such as employment, harvesting crops, or the performance of the family car.

The cycle of anticipation and disappointment which I face, however, relates to my living and dying, or my participation in the life and work of the church. We are not strong enough to face such basic disappointments by ourselves, nor can we work through them once and expect it to last. We need to come to God each time. Daily suffering needs daily grace and encouragement.

Epilogue

Epilogue

Papa died on February 6, 1979, one-and-a-half years after he first became aware of his bout with cancer. At the time of his death, the manuscript for the chapters you have just read waited patiently in his briefcase. There were notes in the margins and hints of new paragraphs awaiting one more review and synthesis on a day when Papa had enough energy.

This small book is one of Papa's dreams, a testimony to his irrepressible exploration of God and life, even in the face of death. Dying, for Papa, was a stimulus—a stimulus for deep inward probing, intensive Bible study, open conversation, and a renewed dependence on God's enduring love. Paradoxically, dying became a stimulus to life. The result was a healthy man, a man whose health in mind and spirit triumphed over a weakening body.

Visiting my father during the last days, hours, and minutes of his life was like being allowed to take a gentle trip through his very soul. Whatever was there—fear, tears, or a deep enduring joy—we were allowed to touch and see. He was blessed with a keen mind that kept searching, and his characteristic spark of humor continued to flourish.

On our last afternoon together, Papa led us in singing songs which had become especially meaningful to him through his illness. We sang "Leaning on the Everlasting Arms," "I Will Bless the Lord at All Times," and "Thy Lovingkindness Is Better Than Life." Singing was an inspiration to him. Watching him sing on through the tears, suffering, and fear, made us aware that we were watching a miracle of the grace of God.

Papa asked us to read two Scriptures after we had finished singing. We read John 14 and John 10. When we read the verse, "I have come that they may have life, and have it to the full." (John 10:10), Papa said something which describes the way we often approach our faith. "Ah yes, we want the life, but oh God, spare us the pain!"

The songs and Scriptures inspired him with more thoughts. He continued, "If I could preach a couple sermons across the church, I know what I'd preach. I'd preach that we need to get the basic truth of God's Word into our system so that whatever emergency in life we meet, we'd have that to fall back on. I'd also tell them this. It's good to learn the biblical truths and enjoy singing the beautiful songs of faith. But we have to keep in mind that when we face the trial of our faith, or look death squarely in the eye, saying the words of truth or singing the songs of faith will not guarantee that we will have the fortitude to walk through the Valley of Death. Only the grace of God Himself is sufficient for that."

If there is one thing which Papa learned in his last days, it is that the grace of God is our ultimate sustainer. Understanding and reason are tools to use as we respond to crises in our lives, but they are not sufficient in themselves. Earlier in our visits he had remarked, "I'd have been better off a long time ago if I had known you can't always figure things out. It's about time I read my own book again, especially that part about *helplessness is not worthlessness*. It was a good insight when I discovered it, but now it's hard to apply."

One thing which we as a family learned through Papa's death is that we need a different definition of health. Even as Papa was dying, his songs, prayers, questions, and faith convinced us that he was a healthy man by all standards that were important. The word "health" is often used in a restrictive sense to apply only to the body. We need to begin thinking of health in a broader sense which includes body, soul, mind, and spirit. Many people who may be able to pass a physical fitness test aren't very healthy. Others whose bodies are weak from suffering may be quite healthy in mind and spirit.

During his illness, Papa drew much of his "health" and strength from family and friends who buoyed his spirits time and time again. Shortly after his initial hospitalization in 1977 Papa reflected on a visit from friends from the Louisville Mennonite Fellowship: "When I reached out for help, I didn't touch a cold stone wall, but the warmth and support of my brothers and sisters." On the eve of his death, I was writing a letter to family and friends concerning his illness. "Be sure to include something about mother's fortitude," he said, "I'm just amazed by her strength."

Our family conversations about death with Papa were a tremendous source of strength for all of us while he lived, and now provide us a sense of comfort and peace since his death. Death is ultimately a lonely experience. Talking about death won't take it away or make it painless. We sensed, however, that our conversations with Papa about his own dying became channels of God's grace for all of us.

Titus Peachey
Son

The
Author

The Author

Mark Peachey (1916-1979) grew up as a farm boy in the hills of southwestern Pennsylvania. In 1939 he married Fannie Beitzel and began a career in farming. He was ordained to the ministry in September 1946 at Oak Dale Conservative Mennonite Church, near Salisbury, Pennsylvania, to serve the Casselman River congregation of Somerset County, Pennsylvania, and Garrett County, Maryland.

Along with his ministerial and farming responsibilities, he did part-time secretarial work for the Conservative Mennonite Board of Missions and Charities (later named Rosedale Mennonite Missions), studied a year at Eastern Mennonite College, and served on the faculty of the Conservative Mennonite Bible School in Berlin, Ohio.

In 1957 Mark, Fannie, and their three children moved from their home at Grantsville, Maryland, to Plain City, Ohio. There he became pastor and bishop of the United Bethel Mennonite Church and later bishop of Burnside Community Mennonite Church in Columbus, Ohio.

His part-time job as secretary to Rosedale Mennonite Missions eventually became a full-time position. During his twenty-five years of service under that Board he was involved in a great deal of traveling, both in the United States and overseas. This broad exposure fostered an openness to new ideas and a sensitivity to people's feelings. He devoted many hours to counseling, especially with young people going into Voluntary Service or other mission assignments. Christian hospitality was a daily part of Mark and Fannie's life together.

In 1974 Mark began a sabbatical leave from Rosedale Mennonite Missions. At 58 years of age he studied for six months at Eastern Mennonite Seminary.

The last four years of his life were spent as pastor of Louisville Mennonite Fellowship in Louisville, Kentucky. It was there that he learned that he was suffering from myelofibrosis. For a year and a half following the diagnosis, he continued as pastor, constantly adjusting to his limitations. He continued thinking, learning, praying, hoping, and counseling—sometimes from his hospital bed—until the day of his death on February 6, 1979.